Railways in B

on old picture

Sandy Cl.

1. The worst accident ever to occur in Bedfordshire happened at about 4am on Thursday, 4th February 1909 at Sharnbrook. This was recorded on a montage postcard published by Warner Gothard of 6 Eldon Street, Barnsley (see front cover). The brief description states *"the 10.05 pm Wednesday, February 3rd Express Goods, Manchester-London travelling about 60 miles per hour, dashed into a Goods Train standing in Sharnbrook Station. The Driver & Fireman of the Manchester Express were buried in the wreckage and killed; their bodies not being recovered until 13 hours afterwards."* A memorial was erected in Sharnbrook cemetery to Arthur Coope (Driver) and John Hawley (Fireman) by their fellow workmen. This card was posted at Bedford a few days after the accident.

Designed and published by
Reflections of a Bygone Age,
Keyworth, Nottingham 2000

Printed by Adlard Print
& Reprographics Ltd

£3.50

Introduction

Bedfordshire is one of the smaller English counties, still mainly rural in character, with Bedford and Luton (including Dunstable) the only towns of any size.

There are two principal railway routes passing through the county north to south, both serving London, namely the former Midland Railway (MR) from the industrial Midlands, and the former Great Northern Railway (GNR) from north-east England.

A further great trunk route, the London and North Western Railway (LNWR) just touches the most westerly part of the county in the Leighton Buzzard area on its way from the north west of England and the West Midlands to London.

Numerous branch lines were also built, wandering across the county in a general east to west direction linking the main trunk routes. The latter still exist, but with the exception of the Bedford to Bletchley line, the branches had all disappeared by the end of the 1960's.

Picture postcards were first published in this country in 1894, but it was not until 1902 that the Post Office allowed the message to be written on the back alongside the address. This led to a boom in picture postcard production and usage - the "Golden Age" of postcards - which lasted up to the end of the First World War (1918). Most local scenes featured on postcards, and railway stations, accidents, staff and buildings were always popular with publishers. National firms to issue picture postcards included W.H. Smith, which published views of all their station bookstalls, the Locomotive Publishing Co., which specialised in the genre, and Valentine of Dundee. Locally, Blake & Edgar and F. Sweetland were responsible for publishing several of the cards featured in this volume. Publishers of all the cards are noted in the captions where known.

Sandy Chrystal
December 2000

Acknowledgments: I would like to thank Andrew Swift for his help and encouragement, and Ken Dickens for unravelling details of the pre-grouping intricacies of the railways of Bedfordshire. Thanks, too, to Ken Fairey, Les Hanson and Robert Humm for permission to reproduce their images.

Back cover (top): Midland Station staff at **Luton** standing on the 'up' platform in 1907. The card was published by T. Marston, stationer, of North Finchley. The station master in 1907 was Samuel Green, but it is unlikely that he is shown here as station masters normally wore bowler hats! In 1907 Luton had a population estimated at 39,000. However, population growth was very rapid in the 1920's and early 1930's, so that the whole station was rebuilt in the mid 1930's to cope with increased traffic.

(bottom): **Sandy** Station looking north c. 1910.

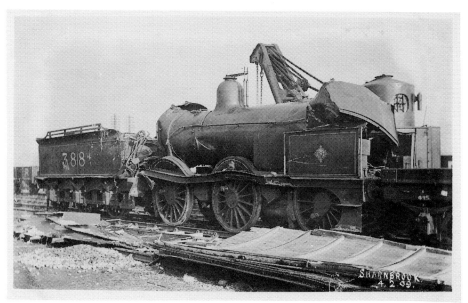

2-3. Two more postcards showing the accident. Both were published by F. Sweetland of Bedford.

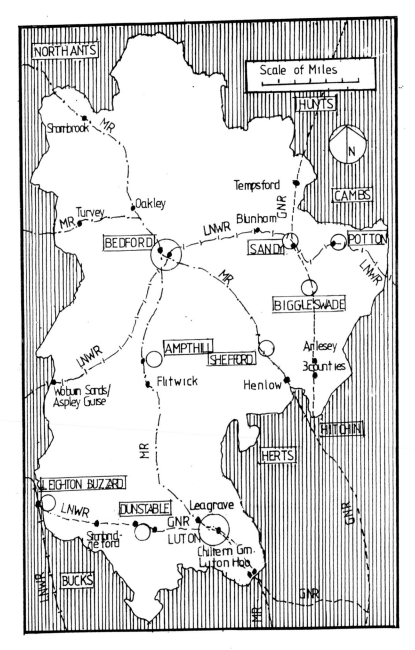

Railways in Bedfordshire on 31st December 1922, the day before Britain's system was grouped into four major companies. Only those stations featured in this book are indicated. I haven't yet found picture postcards of other stations!

SHARNBROOK STATION.

4. **Sharnbrook** station in happier times on a postcard published in Blake & Edgar's "Picturesque Bedfordshire" series. This view is looking south in the Bedford direction.

5. The exterior of **Sharnbrook** station buildings and the house of John Hawkins, the station master. The four-wheeler waiting for passengers probably came from the nearby "Railway Hotel" and posting house which had open and closed carriages to let (it is now "The Fordham Arms"). Postcard sent from Bedford in May 1909.

6. Between Sharnbrook and Bedford is **Oakley** station. This card, published by F. Sweetland of Bedford in about 1910, shows a typical layout similar to Sharnbrook with a terrace of six railway houses to the left beyond the slow (freight) lines.

7. It is somewhat ironic that Oakley junction, only four miles from Sharnbrook, was the scene some thirty years later of yet another bad railway accident. It happened on January 21st 1938 when a London (St Pancras) - Sheffield express ran into a train of empty stock. Les Hanson captured the remains of the damaged locomotive and dining car of the express the following day on postcards.

8. Another Hanson view of the accident. I was a boy of 11 at the time and I have a clear memory of my father, who was working in the vicinity, telling me of the screams of the kitchen staff in the dining car from the boiling water and fat of the food being prepared.

9. This is a general internal view looking north of **Bedford (Midland Road)** Station, published c. 1906 by Valentine of Dundee, one of the most prolific of all British postcard publishers. The light and graceful cast-iron structures with glass infilling which form the platform roofs were known to railwaymen by the Portuguese word "verandah" and are found on most of the larger stations of the Midland Railway (the wired glass was removed during the Second World War for safety reasons).

10. The bookstall on the "up" London platform. The reverse of the card has a *"W H Smith & Son, Bedford Railway Station"* handstamp and the photographer was F. Sweetland, who had a studio at 79 Harpur Street, Bedford in 1910. The bookshop staff standing proudly in front include the bowler-hatted manager. The young lad on the left wears a cap and an Eton collar, and on a wicker tray has a display of magazines which were for sale as he walked up and down the platform.

11. Another view of **Bedford** Station about 1900 with a Samuel Johnson 'Single' no. 171. Card published by The Locomotive Publishing Co. Ltd, 3 Amen Corner, London EC.

12. General view of **Bedford** Station about 1930.

7th A + S H leaving Bedford Dec 11.14

13. In the summer of 1914 the quiet county town of Bedford changed character almost overnight with the start of World War One and the arrival of thousands of Highland troops. They were billeted in private houses all over Bedford and Kempston, as well as living under canvas in the public parks and the grounds of country houses. They spent the remaining months of 1914 getting fit and being trained for the battles to come. Temporary railway sidings and platforms were built next to the Midland mainline off Ampthill Road to receive them, and for their departure to London and the Channel ports. Here we see the 7th battalion of the Argyll & Sutherland Highlanders leaving on December 11th 1914. No doubt many a heart was broken. In fact my father was one of the "Jocks", as they were called, coming from Aberdeen in 1914 to Bedford where he met a Kempston girl. He went through the whole war in Flanders with the Royal Engineers, returned to Kempston and they were married. This postcard was published by Blake and Edgar, 38-40 High Street, Bedford.

14. All the railway companies, including the Midland, issued postcards for publicity purposes. The range was enormous and in the case of the MR went to many sets. One set of six cards covers Bedford and Elstow, including this one featuring Old Newnham Bridge, Bedford.

15. Bunyan's Statue, Bedford, on a card in the same series posted from London in May 1904. They were published by Photochrom, London.

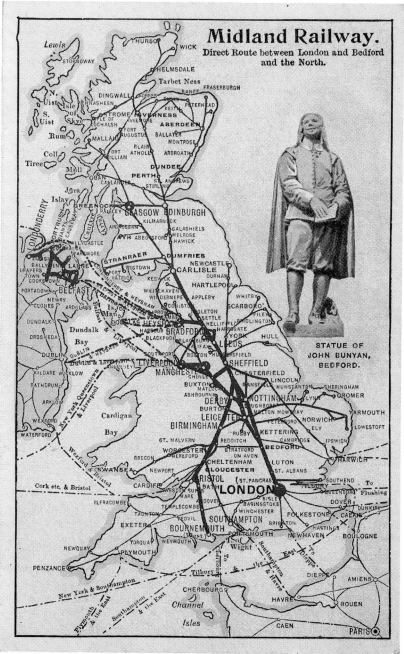

Midland Railway.

Direct Route between London and Bedford and the North.

STATUE OF
JOHN BUNYAN,
BEDFORD.

16. Another series shows a card with a route map of the Midland Railway and Bunyan's Statue.

Midland Railway.

The most picturesque route through
England.
The most interesting route to Scotland.

Recreation Grounds, Bedford.

17. An early postcard published by The British & Colonial Auto Trading Co., London, and posted from the capital in October 1903. It shows the Recreation Grounds, Bedford, and has an undivided back, which was reserved exclusively for the address and adhesive stamp - the message had to be on the picture side, so the picture was often a vignette. Undivided backs persisted until late in 1902.

18. Ampthill Station about 1910. The station master was Robert Turner and he had a staff of seven. Adverts on the station include promotions for Pears soap and Robertson's "Golden Shred."

19. Another view of **Ampthill** in 1915 with the first draft of the Duke of Bedford's Regiment leaving for France on June 9th. The station and its buildings no longer exist.

20. The local stopping train has just left Ampthill Station travelling north to Bedford with the entrance to Ampthill tunnel just visible beyond the graceful arches to the road bridge to Little Park Farm.

21. Flitwick Station looking north as seen on a postcard in Blake & Edgar's *"Picturesque Bedfordshire"* series. The card was posted from Ampthill at 7.30pm on November 9th 1906. The typical red brick station buildings of this stretch of the Midland mainline are still in use, but otherwise it is very different now, with a large car park behind and to the north for commuters, and of course the overhead power cables to service the electrification as far as Bedford.

22. The exterior of **Leagrave** Station, some two and a half miles north west of Luton. Leagrave is the source of the River Lea, a tributary of the Thames, and serves the large residential area that is now part of north Luton. Note the unmade roadway.

23. A postcard of the interior and platforms at **Leagrave**.

24. General view of **Luton Midland** Station from the south west, showing a variety of public and private horse-drawn transport awaiting the arrival of passengers. The background of numerous trees is, of course, totally changed today.

25. **Chiltern Green** Station is almost an exact replica of Leagrave. It was the station for Luton Hoo stately home, and was the final station in the Bedfordshire section of the Bedford-London line built by the Midland Railway and opened in 1868. The station no longer exists, and the main building is now a house. Before the Bedford-London mainline was opened, the route to London was via Hitchin and thence over the Great Northern lines to London (Kings Cross), an unsatisfactory arrangement! However, the old line was retained as a branch line until 1962 when it closed.

G. H. STONEBRIDGE, PUBLISHER.   4, MIDLAND ROAD, BEDFORD.
The Midland Train, Bedford and Hitchin, passing through the flood,
at Bedford, April 30th, 1908.

26. This postcard shows a passenger train hauled by a tank engine passing through the floods on the south side of Bedford on 30th April 1908. These resulted from a very heavy snowfall on the 24th and then a quick thaw, which led to the River Ouse bursting its banks and widespread flooding. The card was sent to Master Poole in Bromley, Kent on May 9th 1908. Card published by G.H.Stonebridge, 4 Midland Road, Bedford.

27. A view of **Southill** about forty years ago, with a typical Midland Railway station signal box on the right and the station building in the distance beyond the siding on the left. Postcard by Ken Fairey.

Henlow Station.   111283.

28. Henlow Station in the early 1930's giving a good view of the stationmaster's house, the public waiting rooms and the ticket office. From the 1920's onwards, the station also served RAF Henlow, transporting personnel and goods for the training of airmen and the repair and maintainance of aircraft.

TURVEY STATION.

29. A card published by B. Wiggins & Son of **Turvey**, show
to Northampton. This was opened by the Midland Railway
to the Bedford-Northampton road about three quarters of
requested in the period just before World War One. The st

om Oakley Junction, two miles north of Bedford heading
he station at **Turvey** was completed in 1872. Sited close
he village centre, cabs of George Osborne met trains as
at that time (with bowler hat) was John Westcott.

THE BIRD IN HAND. — HENLOW STATION BEDS.

30. The" Bird In Hand" public house adjoining the station. The publican standing in the doorway was W.J. Kineton (presumably with his wife and daughter and a couple of regulars). The postcard is in Blake & Edgar's "Picturesque Bedfordshire" series, posted on September 1st 1910 and addressed to Mr Hawkins, Cherry Tree, Bedford, with the message *"Kindly note piano out of order. Yours etc W.J. Kineton"*. The "Cherry Tree" referred to was at 17, Cauldwell Street, Bedford and the lack of a number and name of street shows how well the postmen knew their Bedford pubs!

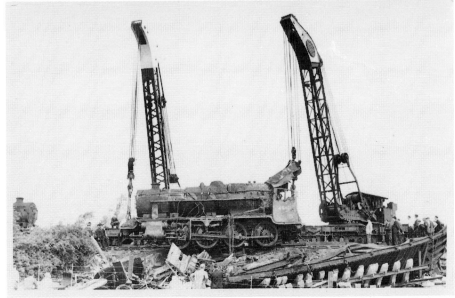

31. Trouble on the line forty years ago! Locomotive 8F no. 48616 being rerailed on July 31st 1960 after running into some stored coaches at Turvey, as seen on a card published by K. Fairey.

32. Railway buffs will tell you that **Leighton Buzzard** Station on the LNWR line from London (Euston) to the north is not actually in Bedfordshire, or indeed Leighton Buzzard. The county boundary with Buckinghamshire is the River Ouzel and the station is in Linslade, thus being a quarter of a mile inside Bucks! However, I am sure that the four likely lads on this postcard would not be bothered by the finer points of topography.

33. Leighton Buzzard's first railway station (1838) on a photographic postcard by P.J. Baker, Leighton Buzzard. Kelly's Directory 1848 mentions that George N. Rich was superintendent of the railway station. However, earlier directories (Pigot & Co. 1839 and Robson's 1839), do not give any details of staff, but give information of train departures.

S.16201. RAILWAY STATION, LEIGHTON BUZZARD.

34. A general view of **Leighton Buzzard** Station in LMSR days, seen on a postcard published by W.H. Smith. This is a late 1920's view, and features some rather elderly taxis!

35. The LNWR branch line from Leighton Buzzard to Dunstable, with a view of the station at **Stanbridgeford,** the only station between the two towns, about forty years ago.

36. Many private company wagons were to be seen on freight trains. Here is one of the Dunstable Lime Co., which had its offices and quarry at Houghton Regis, a mile north of Dunstable, with sidings and a direct connection to the LNWR.

37. The line passed on the north side of Dunstable with two stations (Dunstable North, LNWR and Dunstable Town, GNR) before heading off to Luton (Bute Street) Station on the GNR line. The postcard view of **Dunstable Town** Station shows bleak Blow's Down in the distance. It was posted at Dunstable in August 1914.

OUR LOCAL EXPRESS
Luton to Dunstable
and back same day

38. The comic postcard of "Our Local Express" by the Cynicus Publishing Co. is not for railway aficionados, but shows that even in 1910, when it was posted in Leighton Buzzard, people were making fun of railways. In fact, Bradshaw's 1910 Railway Guide shows a total of eighteen trains per weekday in each direction on the five and a half mile stretch of line.

39. Luton (Bute Street) Station in British Rail days on a postcard by Lens of Sutton.

40. Luton (Bute Street) Station in Great Northern Railway days, with the hearse and coffin of Sir Julius Wernher of Luton Hoo. Postcard published by Chas. R Crawley, 20 Castle Street, Luton.

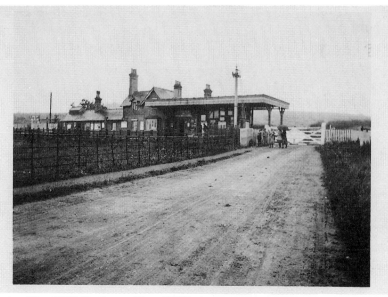

41. Luton Hoo GNR Station at New Mill End, one and a half miles from Luton Hoo. It adjoined MR Chiltern Green Station. View looking south-west.

42. A postcard view of a train on the old GNR near Luton Hoo Station in LNER days. The old Midland Railway (LMSR) is clearly visible in the background. Postcard published by W.S. Garth, 15 Dunstable Rd, Luton.

The Station.

Woburn Sands.

7.

43. The LNWR line from Bletchley in Buckinghamshire to Bedford was opened in 1846, the first rail link that Bedford had to London and Birmingham. This view shows **Woburn Sands** Station with the Dunstable-Newport Pagnall road and level crossing. The postcard was posted on 31st May 1909, but the scene is probably a little earlier.

44. A view from the reverse direction, on a card published by Blake & Edgar.

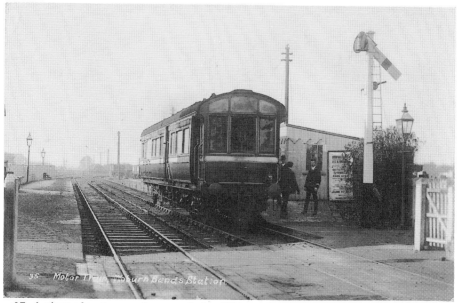

45. A view of a steam rail car posted in Woburn Sands on 28th October 1915. Lily writes to Hilda in Weybridge, Surrey, saying: *"I got home safely at three o'clock and was very glad too as I was tired of sitting in the train"*. Postcard produced for J. Pikesley, Post Office, Woburn Sands in the 'Wells' series.

46. Aspley Guise motor halt just a mile east of Woburn Sands.

47. Bedford (St Johns) Station about 1910, looking east with a freight train heading in the opposite direction to Bletchley.

48. Millbrook as seen by H.B. Priestley's camera forty years ago. The station building is similar in design to Woburn Sands.

49 & 50. Evacuees arriving at **St Johns** Station in 1939 at the outbreak of World War Two. Most family houses in the town had evacuees living with them.

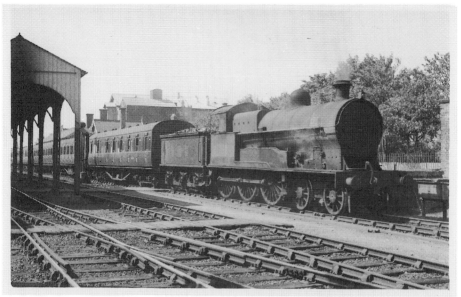

51. A Cambridge-bound train leaving **St Johns** Station on 28th August 1940 ('Prince of Wales Class' engine no. 25694). Postcard published by W.A. Camwell.

52. The station staff at **Blunham** in LNWR days. It is interesting to compare the solid brick style of this stretch of the line through to Potton with the romantic early Victorian half-timber of Woburn Sands and Millbrook *(illus. 43 & 48)*.

53. Sandy Station (LNWR) before closure in 1968 on a postcard by Robert Humm. The line from Sandy to Potton was built by Sandy resident Captain Peel and was opened on 23rd June 1857. Note particularly the very ornate cast iron work of the verandah supports.

54. View of a passenger train to Cambridge from the footbridge at **Potton.**

55. General view of **Potton** Station looking towards Sandy, with the footbridge and the Potton-Sandy road bridge behind. Postcard by Lens of Sutton.

56. The Great Northern Railway, opened in 1850, occupied a stretch of fifteen and a half miles due north-south in flat East Bedfordshire on its way to Kings Cross London. **Tempsford** Station, a mile to the east of the Great North Road, is typical of the smaller stations, with the fast lines in the middle and slow freight lines to the extreme left and right of the island platforms.

57. Sandy Station looking north, with the Sandy-Potton road bridge in the middle distance. The footbridge links the platforms of both the GNR and LNWR stations. The fact that the GNR line was reduced to two lines through Sandy Station caused a troublesome bottleneck. The carriages on the right are on a Bedford-bound train.

58. Sandy Station looking south from the road bridge with an 'Atlantic' no. 1416 heading a train to Peterborough, seen on a card posted in 1912. The LNWR station is on the left, with the distant hill of Sandy Warren behind.

59. Another view of **Tempsford** Station, with stationmaster Edward Smith (second from the right) and staff posing in about 1910.